The BOY WHO LOVED LOVED MATH

The Improbable Life of Paul Erdős

347

29

11

173

47

LOVED MATH

19

The Improbable Life
of **Paul Erdös**

97

61

by **Deborah Heiligman**

pictures by
LeUyen Pham

569

73

SCHOLASTIC INC.

5 13 17 23 41 67 7

There once was a boy who loved math. He grew up to
be 1 of the greatest mathematicians who ever lived.
And it all started with a big problem . . .

79   107   113   139   149   157

Paul Erdős lived in Budapest, Hungary, with his mama. Mama loved Paul to infinity. Paul loved Mama to ∞, too! When he was 3, Mama had to go back to work as a math teacher. She didn't want anything bad to happen to Paul. So she left him with the 1 person she knew would take very good care of him. She left him with . . .

Fräulein!

Fräulein had too many rules.

That was the problem.
Paul hated rules.

He hated to be told
when to sit still,

when to eat,

when to go to sleep.

What could Paul do?

He couldn't exactly solve the problem. But Paul knew that when summer came, Mama would be home with him all day, 100% of the time. So he taught himself to count—really high. Then he figured out how many days it would be until summer vacation. It made him feel much better to know the number.

So Paul kept counting . . .
And thinking about numbers. One day, when he was 4,
Paul asked a visitor when her birthday was. She told him.

What year were you born? he asked.
She told him.

What time?
She told him.

Paul thought for a moment.
Then he told her how many seconds
she had been alive.

1,009,152,358

Paul liked that trick. He did it often.

11
10
9
8
7
6
5
4
3
2
1
0 — — — — — zero — — — —
-1
-2
-3
-4
-5
-6
-7
-8
-9
-10
-11

Paul played with numbers. He added them together and subtracted them. One day he subtracted a bigger number from a smaller number.

The answer was less than 0.

How could a number be < 0?

Mama told him numbers below

are called NEGATIVE NUMBERS. Paul thought that was so cool.

Now he knew for sure he wanted to be a mathematician when he grew up. But first he had to tackle another big problem . . .

School! Mama sent him to school, of course, when it was time. But Paul and school were not a good match. Paul could not sit still for long. So he got up and ran around the classroom. But that was against the rules.

Oh, how Paul hated rules. How could he solve this problem?

Paul told Mama he didn't want to go to school anymore. Not for **1** more day, for **0** days. He wished he could take days away—negative school days! He pleaded with Mama to stay home.

Luckily Mama was a worrier. She worried about germs a lot. She worried Paul could catch dangerous germs from the children at school.

So she helped him solve his problem. She said he could stay home with—

Fräulein!

But even Fräulein was better than school.

Maybe 500 times better . . .

   Fräulein and Mama did everything for Paul.

They

cut his meat

and buttered his bread

and got him dressed

and tied his shoes.

That was great. It meant Paul could think about numbers all day. Numbers were his best friends. He could always depend on numbers to be there and behave in the same way. Numbers followed rules. He didn't like rules in life, but he liked rules in numbers. And so Paul turned 7, then 8, then 9. And when Paul was 10, he fell in love . . .

He fell in love with

PRIME NUMBERS.

Prime numbers are special.
They can't be divided evenly.
A prime number can be
divided only by itself and 1.

The first prime number is 2,
but that is the only even prime number.

All the other prime numbers are odd.
The numbers 3, 5, and 7 are prime.

But not all odd numbers are prime.
9 isn't prime because you can
multiply 3×3 and get 9.

$$P = A + 1 = (2 \times 3 \times 5 \times 7 \times 11 \times \ldots \times P_N) + 1$$

2   37   47   101   23   5   113   7   3   19   29   11   13   17   79   83   131

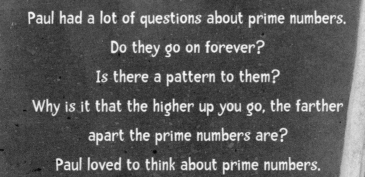

Paul had a lot of questions about prime numbers.

Do they go on forever?

Is there a pattern to them?

Why is it that the higher up you go, the farther apart the prime numbers are?

Paul loved to think about prime numbers.

13

When he got older, Paul wanted to go to high school.

He liked school a $1,000,000$ times better now. He made many friends, people his age who loved math and were really good at it, too.

$$n < p < 2n$$

ANONYMUS
GLORIOSISSIMI BELA REGIS NOTARIVS

Paul and his friends did math together all over Budapest.

But Paul was the best.

He loved being at the top in math

and at the top of towers

and mountains

and buildings, too.

He thought about math

whatever he was doing,

wherever he was.

$$S_r^{(3)} = O + \binom{r}{1}1 + \binom{r}{2}7 + \binom{r}{3}12 + \binom{r}{4}6 = \left[\frac{r(r+1)}{2}\right]^2$$

R(3,3)

By the time Paul was 20, he was already famous around the world for his math. People called him The Magician from Budapest.

But he still did not know how to . . .

do his laundry

or cook his food

or butter his bread.

That was not a problem.
He still lived at home and
Mama still did everything for him.

But then one day, . . .

when Paul was 21, some mathematicians invited him to go to England to work on his math. Could he survive out in the world on his own?

He rode the train by himself.

He met the mathematicians. They all went to dinner.

Everyone else talked and ate, but Paul stared at his bread. He stared at his butter. He didn't know how to butter his bread.

Finally he took his knife, put some butter on it, and spread it on his bread. Phew. He did it! "It wasn't so hard," he said.

Even though he could now butter his own bread, Paul soon realized that he didn't fit into the world in a regular way.

He wasn't the kind of person to cook or clean or drive a car or have a wife and children.

He wasn't the kind of person to live in 1 place and have 1 job.

He was the kind of person to do math.
All of the time.
And he still didn't like to follow rules.

So he invented his own way to live.

Here is what he did:

Paul would get on an airplane with two small suitcases filled with everything he owned—a few clothes and some math notebooks. He might have $20 in his pocket. Or less.

$$g(n) = \Omega(n^{1/2})$$

$$g(n) = \Omega(n^{2/3})$$

$$g(n) = \Omega(n^{((48-14e)/(55-16e))-e})$$

$$g(n) = \Omega(n^{4/5} \log n)$$

$2(n^{5/7})$

$g(n) = \Omega(n^{4/5})$

$g(n) = \Omega(n^{4/7})$

$g(m) = \Omega(n^{(4e/(5e-1))-e})$

He flew from New York to Indiana and to
Los Angeles. He flew across the world,
from Toronto to Australia.
"I have no home," he declared.
"The world is my home."

And wherever he went, when he got there,
the same thing would happen:

21

A mathematician would meet him
and take him home.

The mathematician and Paul
worked on math.

Paul played with the
mathematician's epsilons.

That's what Paul called children,
because an epsilon is a very small
amount in math.

And just as Mama had done, friends all over the world took care of Paul. They

did his laundry

and cooked his food

and cut open his grapefruit

and paid his bills.

Now, Paul wasn't the easiest houseguest . . .

He made messes . . . big messes . . .
like the time he got impatient and opened
a tomato juice carton by
stabbing it with a knife.

And he often woke up his host at 4:00 in the morning
and said, "My brain is open!" That meant he was ready
to do math.

He wanted to do math about 19 hours a day—every single day.

19 hours × 7 days
a week =
133 hours a week

New York Post SPORTS FINAL

FBI DEFEATS SPY SCARE
3 ALIENS JUST STUDENTS

GOVERNMENT PROPERTY NO TRESPASSING

U.S. BORDER PATROL

One time when he was a young man, he broke a rule that got him into big trouble. He climbed over a fence to look at a radio tower. He got arrested. The police thought he was a spy. The FBI thought he was a spy. So *they* spied on *him* for years after that.

Why did friends all over the world put up with him? And take care of him? Call him Uncle Paul and love him?

Because Paul Erdős was a genius—and he shared his brain. He helped people with their math problems and gave them more problems to do. Plus, he was a math matchmaker. He introduced mathematicians all over the world to one another so they could work together. Paul knew that

MatheMATiCiaN + MATHEMATiCiaN + MATHEMATiCiaN = MORE and BETTeR MATH

Paul and his friends did so much great math! They worked in math called

NUMBER THEORY,

COMBINATORICS,

THE PROBABILISTIC METHOD,

and

SET THEORY.

Paul showed his friends
how to do this math in
new and better ways.

He even started some
new kinds of math.

Some of the math Paul and his friends
worked on gave us better computers and
better search engines on the computer.
Also better codes for spies to use!

Uncle Paul was generous with his brain—and his money, too. Whatever money he had, he gave away. He gave money to poor people and he offered prize money for unsolved math problems.

Even when Paul got very old, he still did math.

He did math while he played chess.

He did math while he drank coffee. Lots and lots of coffee.

He thought about math while he played Ping-Pong with his best friends.

Paul said he never wanted to stop doing math. And he didn't. To stop doing math, Paul said, was to die.

So Paul left this world while he was at a math meeting.

$$P_{n+1} > \frac{c \log n \log n}{(\log \log \log n)^2} \ i.o.$$

$$\frac{1}{55} \sum \frac{1}{n} = \infty \Rightarrow \overline{5} \text{ has } k\text{-AP for all } k$$

$$\text{For all } k, \ r_k(n) = o(n)$$

$$2^{1-\binom{k}{2}} < 1 \Rightarrow \text{no monochromatic } K_n$$

pg o m ld ad ld cd

All over the world mathematicians still talk about and love Uncle Paul. Even people who never met him. They talk about their "Erdős number." If you did math with Paul you get an Erdős number of 1. If you worked with someone who worked with Paul, your Erdős number is 2. People are so proud of their Erdős numbers.

G. W. Peck

George Grätzer

Penny E. Haxell

Alan M. Frieze

Rudolf Ahlswede

Endre Szemerédi

Saharon Shelah

Ravindran Kannan

Lowell Beineke

Paul (Pál) Turán

Ronald J. Gould

Ralph Faudree

Steve Butler

Gyula Y. Katona

Daniel J. Kleitman

Ernst G. Straus

Andrew Chi-Chih Yao

Moshe Rosenfeld

Linda Lesniak

Brian Alspach

Albert Einstein

Dimitris Achlioptas

László Lovász

Imre Bárány

András Hajnal

Joel Spencer

Alfred Tarski

András Sárközy

Stefan A. Burr

Vera T. Sós

Alfréd Rényi

Paul (Pál) Erdős

Solomon W. Golomb

John L. Selfridge

Andrew Granville

Ron Graham

Fan Chung

Cecil C. Rousseau

Carl Pomerance

George Szekeres

Frank Harary

Esther Szekeres

Igor Shparlinski

31

32

A long time ago there was a boy who loved
math. Numbers were his best friends.
He grew up to be the man who loved math.
Numbers and people were his best friends.
Paul Erdős had no problem with that.

33

A Note from the Author

When I was a child I loved math as much as I loved reading and writing. But as I got older, I started to think that math was for other people, not me. So how did I come to write a book about a brilliant and important mathematician? All the credit goes to my sons. My older son, Aaron, loved math from an early age. He asked us to give him math problems for fun. One day he told us about this math pilgrim named Paul Erdős (pronounced AIR-dish). I was intrigued, but when our younger son, Benjamin, who is not what I would call a "math guy," started talking about Erdős, I knew I had to learn more. I fell in love with Paul and his story.

Paul was an unusual person who didn't fit into the world in a "regular" way. Yet he figured out how to have a wonderful and meaningful life with an amazing career and legions of adoring friends. I was touched by his generosity. He was a genius in a field of geniuses who worked alone. That's our image, isn't it, of a mathematician? Working alone in a garret somewhere, scribbling numbers, away from prying eyes. But Paul did not believe in hiding his insights. He shared his genius from person to person, country to country; one of his friends described him as a bee, pollinating math. And because he did share, new fields of math were founded and mathematical research, discoveries, and applications multiplied exponentially. Paul demonstrated that math could be fun and social. If he weren't already depicted as a saint on a church wall (in San Francisco), I'd lobby for it.

Writing a picture book about Paul Erdős was a challenge. Many fascinating details of his story couldn't be included in the book. I had to leave out some sad parts of his life, for instance. Paul Erdős was born in Budapest on March 26, 1913. When Paul's mother was in the hospital ready to give birth to him, his two older sisters died of scarlet fever. Paul's parents were devastated, of course, and later his mother told Paul his sisters had been brilliant—even smarter than he was.

When Paul was three, his father was sent to fight in World War I. He was captured and sent to a prison camp in Siberia—he wasn't able to return home for four years. No wonder his mother, Anyuka, was so protective of Paul! Although Paul's mother was probably the central person in his life emotionally, Paul was close to both of his parents, and his father taught him many things. His father introduced Paul to prime numbers, taught him a lot of other math, and how to speak English and French. (Papa taught himself these languages while he was a prisoner of war.)

Paul made his name by discovering an elegant proof for a theorem by a man named Chebychev. Another mathematician honored Paul by making up this jingle about him: "Chebychev said it, and I'll say it again: There's always a prime between N and 2N!" Paul thought all proofs should be elegant and simple. He liked to imagine that there was a book in which God kept all of the most elegant proofs, and Paul referred to particularly appealing solutions as "book proofs."

Paul made his first trip away from home in 1934, when he traveled to Manchester, England. He did not want to leave Europe, but as the Nazis rose to power, Jewish people, like Paul and his family, were in danger. So Paul's parents insisted that he go to the United States in 1938. Most of Paul's relatives were murdered in World War II; his father died of natural causes during that time. Fortunately, his mother survived.

In 1941, curious Paul climbed over a fence enclosing a radio tower. It was wartime and Americans were suspicious of foreigners. When he was questioned Paul said he didn't see the "No Trespassing" sign because he was thinking about math. That's probably the truth, but the American government didn't see it that way. They thought Paul was a spy. In 1954, during the Cold War, he wanted to attend the International Mathematicians Conference in Amsterdam. He had to obtain a reentry visa to be able to come back to the U.S. When he was questioned, he answered honestly. Some of his answers, innocent though they were (for example that he would travel to Hungary to visit his mother), led the officials to believe he was a threat to the U.S. They said that if he left he would not be allowed back in. He went anyway. (Paul still did not like rules.) He was not allowed back into the U.S. for almost a decade.

Paul's mother lived a long time, and even though they lived in different places most of the time, they stayed close. Sometimes Mama even traveled with him to math meetings.

Paul died at a math meeting in Warsaw, Poland, on September 20, 1996. But he is still inspiring mathematicians. There is some of Paul's prize money left for unsolved problems, and people are still getting Erdős numbers.

As I write this, there are no other books for epsilons about Uncle Paul. Adults can learn more about Paul by reading two excellent books: Paul Hoffman's *The Man Who Loved Only Numbers* and Bruce Schechter's *My Brain Is Open*. And there is a wonderful documentary called *N Is a Number*, which I watched many times. To be able to "meet" Paul Erdős, listen to him talk, and watch him interact with others, is amazing. I think you would enjoy it.

For more information about Paul, including links to websites about Paul Erdős, please visit my website, DeborahHeiligman.com. You will see that Uncle Paul really did not leave us.

A Note From the Illustrator

I had a great amount of fun trying to incorporate the world of math with the world of art in this book. Whenever possible, I tried to include some mathematical concept or theory into a composition, whether in the form of equations, graphs, or number groups. Below is a more detailed explanation of the math I used in some of the images. I hope any mathematicians out there (current or future) will enjoy searching them out!

Paul Erdős had a particular affinity for prime numbers. In my research of them, I've found them absolutely fascinating. Imagine numbers that can't be broken down by any smaller divisor! It's such an intriguing concept that there are whole research groups devoted to searching for the largest primes. At the time this book was created, the largest calculated prime number was 12.9 million digits long, and that number is likely to have increased by the time you read this. How can it be possible that such a large number can't be divided by anything but itself and 1? Throughout the book, in various compositions, I've referred to prime numbers as often as possible.

Page 1 The numbers above young Paul's head are harmonic primes.

Page 2–3 The numbers Paul is reciting are called amicable numbers, which are two different numbers so related that the sum of the proper divisors of each is equal to the other. For example, the number 220 can be divided into 1, 2, 4, 5, 10, 11, 20, 22, 44, 55, and 110. When added together, these numbers equal 284, which can be divided into 1, 2, 4, 71, and 142. These numbers, when added together, equal 220. I think it's a lovely concept and a wonderful way to show the relationship between Paul and his beloved mother.

In the background is the city of Budapest. The numbers assigned to the buildings are types of primes, from left to right: dihedral primes, good primes, Leyland primes, Mersenne primes, prime triplets, unique primes, palindromic primes, Ramanujan primes, and two-sided primes.

Page 4–5 In all my research, I couldn't find a single image of the dreaded Fräulein, so I took some liberties in interpreting her. The picture on the dresser on page 5 is an image of Paul's father, who figured largely into Paul's life even in his absence. Paul's father returned from being a prisoner of war when Paul was still young, and it was he who instilled the love of prime numbers in Paul.

Page 8–9 As a young boy, Paul was known to flap his arms when something particularly excited him. This behavior continued through his teen years, when his friends would often have to explain to passersby that there was nothing wrong with Paul—he was just thinking hard.

Page 10 Paul is reading a mathematical journal printed in Hungary for high schoolers, called *KöMal*. *KöMal* was famous for its articles, but the real draw for students was the contest problems. Students would mail in solutions, and the best ones would be published in the journal. At the end of the year, students who had solved the most problems would have their pictures printed. In 1926, when Paul was just thirteen, his picture was printed in the journal, along with his future fellow mathematicians Paul Turán and Esther Klein.

Page 11 Paul is reciting odd numbers and even numbers. The building they are passing is the Hungarian Academy of Sciences of which Paul would later become an honorary member.

Page 12–13 Paul's father was the first to explain prime numbers to him. To show him that prime numbers are infinite, he offered Euclid's Proof of the Infinity of Prime Numbers, which is the equation that Paul is writing in the lower left hand corner of page 12. On the right is a chart called the Sieve of Eratosthenes, which is a simple algorithm for finding all prime numbers. You simply start with a chart listing numbers as high as you'd like to go. Circling 2, the first prime number, you go across the chart and cross out each multiple of 2. The next number uncrossed will be 3, which is the second prime. You then cross out every multiple of 3. You continue in this manner as high as you like, with the next uncrossed number always being the next prime. This is an easy way of finding primes, although you're limited to how high you can count!

Page 14 On page 14 is an illustration of Paul and his friends Paul Turán, Esther Klein, and George Szekeres discussing math at the Statue of Anonymous, a favorite meeting place for Paul and his friends. The equation Paul is pointing to is his elegant proof of Chebychev's theorem. Simply stated, it says that between any prime number and its double, there is at least one other prime number. For example, between the prime number 2 and its double, 4, is another prime number: 3. Paul discovered this proof when he was a very young man, and his work on this theorem gained him enormous attention.

Page 15 Paul and his friends are seen at various landmarks in Budapest.

The graph on the rooftop of the inner city parish is called Euler's map of Konigsburg, which was a problem that Paul and his friends puzzled over. It asserts that it is impossible to touch each vertice (point on the graph), crossing each edge once, without crossing at least one edge twice.

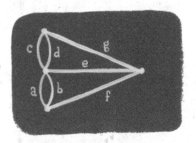

The graph on the rooftop of the University Library is called the Party Problem, which is used to describe Ramsey's theorem.

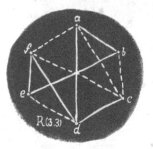

The puzzle states that six people (points a–f) are invited to a party. Some are friends, and some are strangers. Is it true then that among the guests there will always be three people who are all friends or three who are all strangers? To prove this, Paul and his friends used dotted lines and solid lines to represent those who are friends and those who are strangers. To sit down and draw out all the possibilities of this, it would take 32,768 combinations, far too many for any one person to attempt. Instead, Paul and his friends determined that to prove the idea, one simply had to avoid drawing a triangle of either solid lines or dotted lines. After all, a triangle would prove that at least three people (three points on the graph) were either friends or strangers. After a few attempts, they realized that it was impossible to not draw a triangle, thereby proving their theorem.

On the hillside, the equation over Paul's head is taken from one of the first papers he wrote. The graph drawn on the hillside is called a Szekeres Snark, discovered by Paul's friend and fellow mathematician George Szekeres.

Page 16 On the blackboard behind Paul is part of Paul's proof of Issai Schur's conjecture, which led Schur to call Paul "the Magician from Budapest."

Page 18–19 Paul Erdős traveled to England in 1934, after securing a fellowship at the University of Manchester through Louis Joel Mordel, a British number theorist. Page 18 illustrates a stop he made in Cambridge before reaching Manchester. He was met by Harold Davenport, a Cambridge University mathematician, and his wife Anne (in red hat). The other mathematicians pictured in the middle image are Louis Mordel, G. H. Hardy, Chao Ke, and Richard Rado.

While at Cambridge, Erdős challenged his new friends with a puzzle: Can a square be dissected into several smaller squares, each with a different size? Erdős rationalized that it could not be done. Several mathematicians took up the challenge, and Erdős was eventually proven wrong. Page 19 illustrates one of those solutions, discovered by A. J. W. Duijvestin in 1978.

Page 20–21 The equations listed on this page are the partial results of the Erdős distinct distances problem, which states that between a number of distinct points on a plane (n) there are at least $n^{1-0(1)}$ distinct distances. The graphs found on this page are more samples of graph problems posed by Paul and his friends.

Page 22 The mathematician seen here seated with Paul is Stanislaw Ulam, who contributed enormously to research in thermonuclear weapons and nuclear pulse propulsion. Ulam's daughter, Claire, was one of the many children Paul played with on his travels. One of his favorite tricks was dropping a coin or a pill bottle from a certain height, and then quickly catching it before it hit the ground. He performed this trick of agility well into old age, much to the delight of the children he would meet.

Page 23 The mathematicians shown are (in clockwise position) Paul Turán, Alfréd Rényi, Ron Graham, and Fan Chung.

Page 24–25 The mathematician in the upper left is János Pach, who recounted the tomato juice story in the book *The Man Who Loved Only Numbers* by Paul Hoffman. Moshe Rosenfeld is the mathematician below that, who told me that Paul had done this to me on occasion. On page 25, the headline from the *New York Post* is the actual headline used at the time of the story, though the image is my own fabrication.

Page 27 The mathematicians depicted are (reading clockwise) Paul Erdős, András Szemerédi, George and Esther Szekeres, Melvyn Nathanson, Jaroslav Nešetřil, László Lovász, Béla Bollobás, Daniel Kleitman, Péter Frankl, Vojtěch Rödl, Fan Chung, Ron Graham, Joel Spencer, and Vera Sós.

Page 28 The image in the upper left corner of Paul giving money to a beggar is taken from an account by D. G. Larman, who says "Erdős came to visit us for a year. After collecting his first month's salary he was accosted by a beggar on Euston station, asking for the price of a cup of tea. Erdős removed a small amount from the pay packet to cover his own frugal needs and gave the remainder to the beggar."

The mathematician playing Ping-Pong with Paul is László Lovász.

Page 29 The letters PG OM LD AD LD CD refer to a joke that Paul would often use in his lectures to describe himself. The initials stand for "Poor Great Old Man Living Dead Archaeological Discovery, Legally Dead, Counts Dead."

Page 30-31 In my research for this book, I stumbled across a sketch (see below) drawn by Ronald Graham. It is an early incarnation of the Erdős number in graph form and helped to turn Paul Erdős into a cult figure for the mathematical world. I found it such a lovely gesture as well, that the man whose life had been devoted to math could himself be the center of such a complicated graph, and it was the inspiration for the drawing on these pages.

Page 32–33 The buildings here are all covered in prime numbers. The children's t-shirts show the symbol for epsilon.

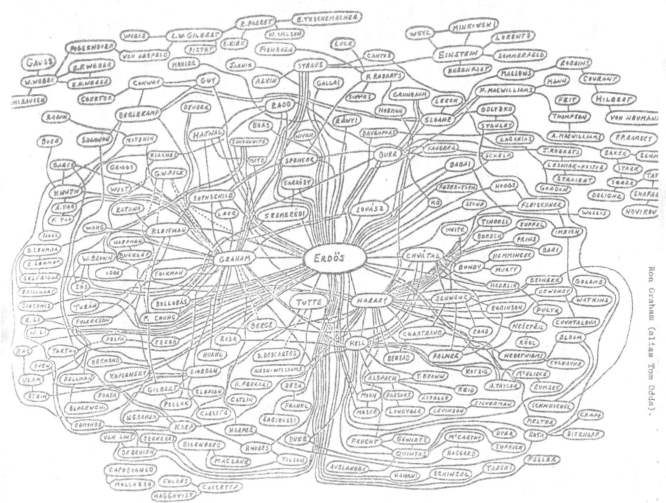

© Ronald Graham

Ron Graham (alias Tom Odda).

Author acknowledgments

Googolplex thanks to these friends of Paul who shared their brains and their memories with me: Ron Graham, Vera Sós, Fan Chung, Andrew Woldar, János Pach, Ralph Faudree, Jerrold Grossman, Prasad Tetali, Richard Schelp, Ioana Dumitriu, Seymour Benzer, and Debbie Golomb. A special thanks to Joel Spencer. He is a kind and brilliant mathematician, with an Erdős number of 1! Having him help me as I wrote and revised was a writer's dream. Former epsilon Barbie Benzer shared her memories, photos, and especially her love for Paul with me. A special thank-you to Benjamin's middle school math teacher, Scott Kolodziejski, who has been waiting for this book for 3 x 3.14 years, at least! And to Floyd Glenn for lending me his books and his math mind. Thank you to George Csicsery for his film *N Is a Number* and for sharing the outtakes with me. Thanks to Martha Pichey for the use of her workroom in the back garden at Eton Villas; the creative energy in that room helped me write many drafts of this book. Much gratitude to Nancy Feresten for an insight early on, and to Steve Meltzer and Deborah Brodie for their hard work on this project. I am so sorry Deborah has left this world and is not here to see THE BOY. Thanks to my editor, Deirdre Langeland, who has shepherded THE BOY with loving hands, and to Anne Diebel, whose vision guided all of us, and to Simon Boughton for steering the ship. Infinite thanks to LeUyen Pham for her brilliant and artistic mind and for her devotion to this project. I could not have done this book without Benjamin Weiner and my math men Aaron Weiner and Jerome Weiner. Thanks, also, to my husband, Jonathan Weiner, who is not a math man, but is infinitely generous with his brain, and to Ken Wright, for everything. And finally, to Paul Erdős himself. His life itself is an elegant proof. He will be in "The Book" forever.

Illustrator acknowledgments

In doing the illustrations for this book, I had to call upon many people for their assistance, both mathematical and otherwise. Most have already been mentioned in the previous acknowledgment. In particular, I'd like to thank Ron Graham for his many phone calls, emails, and patience with me. He provided the equations pictured on the blackboard on page 29, and created a sketch that was the inspiration for my artwork on pages 30–31. Ron's main contribution, however, was revealing to me the humanity behind Uncle Paul, which I tried as much as possible to convey in the book. Thank you also to George Csicsery for spending a morning with me reviewing my paintings and sharing inspiration for other projects, to Juliana Park, who braved the bitter February cold of Eastern Europe to explore Budapest with me, and to Brian Faiola, for his satellite research from Budapest. Of course a thank you to Deborah Heiligman, for writing the story that became the most challenging, and most rewarding, of the many books I've illustrated. And to the folks at Roaring Brook (you know who you are), who patiently waited for me to complete this book with hardly a complaint, I am eternally grateful. And a most special thanks to Anne Diebel, who envisioned me for this project when probably nobody else could (myself included!), and who just let me run with it . . .

For Zachary Weiner,

who is inventing his own special way to live

—D.H.

This book is most humbly dedicated to Anne Diebel.

—L.P.

ISBN 978-0-545-70305-5

Text copyright © 2013 by Deborah Heiligman. Illustrations copyright © 2013 by LeUyen Pham.
All rights reserved. Published by Scholastic Inc., 557 Broadway, New York, NY 10012, by arrangement
with Roaring Brook Press, a division of Holtzbrinck Publishing Holdings Limited Partnership. SCHOLASTIC
and associated logos are trademarks and/or registered trademarks of Scholastic Inc.

12 11 10 9 8   17 18 19/0

Printed in the U.S.A.   40

First Scholastic printing, February 2014

347　59　173

331

47　37

29

569

7

71

131

53　521